A BUTTERFLY'S BOOK OF POETRY

GINGER LOUISE

A Butterfly's Book of Poetry

Published in the United States of America

ISBN: 979-8-218-20020-6

DEDICATION

I want to thank my Aunt J for encouraging my love of reading. Thank you to my big sister for letting me read all your Trixie Belden books. Thank you to my boys for the honor of being your mom and for showing me what unconditional love feels like.

I also want to thank MB and Julie. This book wouldn't have happened without their help.

Hey baby girl
Can I bring
You some flowers

And then he told me

I know the boss

Since I was a little girl I just wanted to be held.
Snuggled close by a mom or dad.
When I was a little girl I wanted a friend.
Someone to play and laugh with at the playground.
When I was a young girl I wanted a boyfriend.
Someone to walk hand and hand with at the park.
Someone to hug while I celebrated
or even while I cried.
Since I was a little girl I've just wanted
someone to help me.
Walk with me thru this life.
To love me and always be there when I woke.
Ever since I was little I've never wanted
to be left alone.

When I look in the mirror
Starr is who I see
Not the little girl who was hurt just like me
But the sister who was mean
Did things that
left me bruised and scarred
When I look in the mirror
The monster is always staring back at me

Do you remember what you use to say to yourself
in the adoption line?
Be perfect
Think what do they want me to be
And just be that
Be perfect

Why can't you do that now?

Do you remember what you used to do when you
had to stand on one leg in the orphanage hall?
Pretend to be a statue
Pretend my body was there but not my mind
Pretend to be a bird flying in the clouds
Pretend
Pretend

Why can't you do that now?

When I was a kid I was a scrapper. I was scrawny.
Which to me meant I was fast. Agile.
Could climb anything. Fit through anywhere.
Go. Go. Go.
I never remember being tired.
Hungry yes. Headaches yes. Never tired.
Physical pain was either from a beating
or something sexual.
I never noticed the pain from a scraped knee.
It was a battle wound. Proof of what I could do.

What if I don't meet the expectation
That's the real fear
That damn line in the orphanage
Picked over and examined
Made me a thing not a human
Something to be poked

I Couldn't Say

My new life came with its own language
And own rules of course
Cussing was no longer allowed
Period.
Pussy was out too
I couldn't say ma'am
Butt
Hell
Yonder
Even Appalachia was said a different way
as was Amen and Hundred
Sex was spoken by its 3 letters
S.E.X.

One thing I know for certain about myself
is that I'm a runner
I've run away from countless beatings
I've run and climbed away from so many fights
I've run myself breathless
trying to escape the feelings
I ran around that playground
Pretending I was free
I ran away from home
I've run away from help
I've ran to help
I ran all the way to the tracks
and then couldn't stay on them
I ran from Kansas
What will I run from next?

Dreamt I was lost
In the woods or the jungle
Not sure which
Choking on sweat, humidity, my fear
Running towards or away
Not sure which
Hiding
Hiding
Always hiding
From myself or others
Not sure which

I love lists
They have always been my answer
When I didn't know where to start
Overwhelmed and mind racing
I could sit down and begin
What do I need to do?
Just vomit it all out on paper
and then begin to order it with
Where do I begin?

Lists

I make lists
I love making lists
I've created piles and piles of lists
Paper piles of magazine clippings
and school mailings
Add in the junk mail
I don't know what to do with all the piles
I obsess over how to go thru the piles
I make lists of ideas on how to conquer my
piles of papers
Of half done projects
And looming Have Tos
All this takes up my time and thoughts
I saw a list today of all the things I want to do
None of them can be done while sitting
obsessing over my lists and piles
If I were to conquer these piles I would be left with
Time
I say that's what I want
Time to do all these things
on one of those lists
Time
Time

Time to decide
How do I decide what to do next
if I don't have a pile to think of
Sitting in the beauty of the day
Although top of the list of Want To Do
is really my fear
If my mind were able to be empty
would I feel as empty as I did then?
Can I overcome the emptiness of those days?

When you're young you can't see that far
into the future
The older you get the further you can see
I never thought I would leave
I knew my parents had the money
to pay for me to stay forever
They would always listen
to what the doctors had to say
I gave up on getting out of there
I cut on my face, arms and legs
Anywhere
It didn't matter
Only the crazies were going to see me anyway
I did things because I didn't see further
Didn't see beyond the now of my life
I hung myself with my shoelaces
Then I had no shoes
I sliced my wrists with razor blades
Then I had no privacy
I said horrible things to the people around me
Wanting to hate them all
Yet we were all we had
I made the doctors into the orphanage staff
Keeping me locked up

Maya Angelou showed me I was the only one
with the key
I had locked myself up
Turned it into Them against Me

I once lived in a complex
of one bedroom apartments
The baby crying next door sounded
the same as the one crying next to me
Rosie and Buddy had a Bedroom Only bedroom
The rest of us shared the mattress
that doubled as the Watch T v corner
The kitchen was against the back wall
No stove
Just burners
A green fridge
I imagined having that bedroom all to myself
I imagined
And I prayed
I prayed for a bed of my own
A room of my own
A home of my own
The crew built a guest house in 3 days
A house bigger than any one from my childhood
A house just for visitors
I can't help but cry
I am so thankful
God you heard me
I don't know why but you went beyond
answering my prayer

22

22 days

22 treatments

Not my magical 23

Not that awesome 21

But 22

For 22 days

I woke myself

Dressed myself

Drove myself

(To 22 treatments)

I haven't done that since

Well I guess high school

I mean I'm not counting Kansas

Doing something for myself

Repeatedly

Is almost more significant than the treatments

I showed up

22 times

No canceling

No rescheduling

22 times

I am healed

I can feel it

It took me choosing to go to extreme measures

22 times

Choosing

When I was little I would ask God
Why didn't I die?
Why didn't my psyche or heart break?
When I was a teen I would ask God
Why didn't I die?
Why didn't I just die with any of the attempts?
When I woke this morning I asked God
Why didn't I die?
Why didn't any disease win?

Rosie
I just want to say I'm sorry
I didn't cry as much as I wanted to
I only cried that once
Busy being angry at you
I didn't want you to leave
I wanted you to come back for me
A new mommy came along
I didn't want her to leave
So I pretended you had never been
And she was the best
Which made you the worst
I am so sorry
I loved you
I love you

26 years ago
Saying it aloud sounds just as crazy
as when I hear it in my head
26 years ago today
I gave birth to a little boy
Held him in my arms, sang to him, said goodbye to
him and handed him to the parents I picked for him
Cried for hours after
My scrawny baby-less body shaking until they sedat-
ed me
I knew adoption was the best for him
I knew he deserved more than I could give him
I didn't expect my arms to ache
For him
My heart to long
For him
I am blessed
No sealed records
No hidden secrets
Gave room for our relationship today
My children resemble him
My boys know him
He is alive and healthy
Healthy and Happy

I'm his mom yet I'm not
I'm a grandma yet I'm not
Are genetics anything?
Everything?
There is a technically
Although it doesn't change the reality
I can't just show up on a doorstep
Don't even have an address
I'm in his life even tho I'm not
I gave him up for adoption
So he's nothing?
I'm nothing?
Maybe I'm nothing to him
Maybe
I am a life giver
I am a family starter

20 years ago
I didn't have children
I didn't believe I would
It all was a hope and a dream
I didn't have a house
I didn't believe I would
It all was a hope and a dream
I didn't have a husband
I didn't believe I would
It all was a hope and a dream
I didn't have a life
I didn't believe I would
I was hoping I would
I was dreaming I would

God I made you a promise
A promise I'd like to break
When you found me a family
I promised I would do anything to keep them
I would do whatever they asked of me
I would let them do whatever they wanted to me
Anything to not go back to the orphanage
Anything to not be out on the street
I didn't want them to love me
I didn't even want them to like me
I just didn't want to be alone anymore
I wanted to know what it was like
to call someone dad
I wanted food that wasn't stolen or rotten or raw
Now I see my two boys and I want more for myself
Self-respect and love
A worth that goes beyond food and a bed

I counted today
To not think of them leaving
I counted today
To stop feeling my heart ache as tho they had
already left
I counted the boxes I broke down
I counted the waters as I put them away
I counted the emails I deleted
I counted the clothes I folded
I counted the days they would be gone
I counted the hours until they go
I counted

Heard the cooing today
Had given up on finding peace today
Ha
God showed me
8am the cement truck backed in
Eeeep eeeep eeeep
It only lasted a few hours
My brain heard it for longer
All the workers are gone now
I thought I'd catch the sun setting
Found so much more
The doves on the roof
The hummingbird in the orange colored flowers
This construction will end
All these people will leave
I will be able to once again bask in Arizona's beauty
For now I must take these moments when I can
Flit along with the hummingbird
Imagine myself the butterfly

Drunk off my ass I can finally breathe
Take a moment
Without judgement to see
Just where I've gotten myself
Quicksand swallowing me with every step
But I sought the quicksand
Naively thinking I could tip toe my way through
I'm now up to my neck and still trying to decide
If I'm really in danger

I hold on

I hold on to a lot
Ok ok
I hold on to everything
This is actually a new thought to me
It started this morning
I said to myself
You hold on to every thought don't you
I can spend hours
Days even
Stuck on one thought
Ususally not good ones
But I hold on to them

I hold on to conversations
Ones from today all the way to childhood
I hold on to memories
Every single one
So tightly

I hold on
I hold on to everything
I have every single card ever given to me
since being adopted

I have held on to every birthday, every Christmas,
every Easter, every special occasion card
From everyone

I hold on to rocks from different places
I have one from the orphanage
I hold on to gifts
I have every one my boys have given me
They are now 16 and 14
I hold on
Scraps really right along with
the clothes and the files

I hold on too much
I hold on to dreams I cannot have
I hold on to wishes that cannot come true
I hold on to people who aren't here anymore
I hold on to things that have no meaning anymore
I hold on to fears
I hold on to doubts
I hold on

When I was very small I held on
I held on tight to the bed post
I held on tight to Starr's hand
I held on tight to the hope of one day

I see where my grip has saved me
I hold on
I hold on to survival

Now how do I let go?
Let go of the doubts and the fears?
Let go of the old stories and the
weight of the guilt and shame?
Let go
How do I let go after holding on for so long?

Vulgar Vulva

It must be vulgar
Spoken about in hushed tones
Mine was damaged at 3
Diseased and disfigured
I forgave and forgot
For forty years
Then I was informed it wasn't over yet
It all turned to cancer and now
my vulgarity is being cut away
Slice by slice
Dissected for observation and diagnosis
Bodies are not vulgar
What is done to them is

I am always chasing you
Running after you
Scrambling to find you
The looking for you is getting old
The constant stomach rolls are tiresome
Run ahead
Keep up
Fall behind

It's ok that I love him

It's ok that I left him

It's ok that I want him

It's ok that I learned I don't need him

It's ok that I am scared

It's ok that I am relieved

It's ok that I believed the lies

It's ok that I only saw what I wanted

It's ok

It's ok

It's ok that I had to leave to live

It's ok that I survived

It's ok that I chose my life

It's ok

It's ok

It's ok that I am smiling
It's ok that I am giggling like a kid
It's ok that I feel the freedom
It's ok
It's ok
It's ok that I called the cops
It's ok that I chose my kids not the man
It's ok that I don't know what's next
It's ok
It's ok
It's ok that I just want to hug my boys
It's ok that I am not Rosie and yet I am
It's ok that I can breathe now
It's ok
It's ok

So he isn't who you thought he was

Big deal

Right?

Is anyone

Truly?

Is anything

Truly?

Move on

Say thank you and move on

Sounds so easy

Every song

Every smell

Every scene

A memory

An ache

A fuck you

I want to scream

Learn and move on

Grow and move on

I've moved

Why am I still sad?

Something happened today
I was singing songs of missing you
But I don't
Sighing oh so deeply
I sang louder and louder
Smiling as I realized
I don't
I'm happy without you
I'm more than ok without you
I'm able to breathe without you
Driving and dreaming
Laughing and loving
All without you
I just don't need you
I may still love you
I just don't miss you
I just don't want you

I am clean
My intentions are good
All the dirt that I've seen
All the filth that I've been
I swear I am clean
My intentions are good
I've done the work
Made amends
Asked for forgiveness again and again

Always the fears first
Always the worries and self-doubt
Fill my head and heart
Always flush with shame first
Always cry at first
Always the bad memories before the good
Always hesitation on my part
Always freeze first
Always want to spread love and joy
Always want to learn how
Always want to give thanks
Always have I survived

I'm real
I'm really real
I exist
I must
I took the blood test
And now I know
If I have a blood type I must be real
I must have been born
I must really have a life to live
Somehow the knowing
B positive
I am B positive
I am

I am invisible
I've done it on purpose
I've done it to myself
Hiding from everyone
Maybe even myself
I have no friends
I have no connections
I've been too busy disappearing to make any
It's all been a choice
A way to survive
Now what do I do
I've survived
I'm living

I was hacked
First my credit card
Then my laptop
I was hacked
Horror movie images
Hacked
Chopped
Into little pieces
Me
Scattered about
Discarded

I'm putting myself back together
Changing in this new world without him
Stronger
Happier
I was hacked
I am becoming whole
Starting over
Changing the image I have of myself
Changing my story

I've sliced and carved into my body
Thinking I could end all the pain and
escape into nothingness
I sliced my wrists
Only to be stitched together again
Carved into my stomach my self hatred
They healed into thin white lines
a few raised welts the only reminder
Those were dark years
Years I truly believed would never end or change
I tattooed inner strength on my ankle
A beautiful spiral of continual growth on my finger
I imagine a butterfly someday
Because I have a some day
Those dark years did end
I did survive

It's slick like sweat from a marathon runner
Oil running like a river
Rain rushing down the gutters

That's the image in my head of my anger
Rage boiling up like hot lava
No spewing
No burst
No fireworks
Just a gushing steadiness
Overwhelming me

My soul hurts
All that I allowed
Not thinking I was worthy
I crawled on my knees
All your raging
I sank deeper
Dragged by my hair
I went limp
Like when I was a child
You knew all my triggers
You knew where I'd go
Instead of raising me up with love
You handed me the shovel
I dug my own grave
I'm done with the self pity
I'm done with the wondering why
What matters is you're gone
I'm safe and only going to rise

I didn't brush my teeth today
I did feed the cats
I didn't do my yoga class
I did do my meetings
I didn't get out of bed today
I did tell my boys I love them

Twenty years later
I'm alive
I didn't think I would be
I'm a mom
I didn't think I would be
I'm alive
I didn't think I would be

My boy turns 15 tomorrow
The one who made me a mom
A special bond because I'm just so grateful God
gave me another chance
He's the child I didn't think I'd have
He's the one I had waited 11 years for
I think about all my wishes and dreams
I'm most grateful to have been apart
of this amazing person's life so far
To have been able to have
such a wonderful relationship
To a real person
Not the one I prayed for
For this is not my prayer standing before me
It's him and his life

I walked the path today
For the first time since buying this house
It's different than the path at my last home
That one was flat right angles and straight
This one meanders around waterfalls
and the remaining mesquite
Over a green painted bridge and a root
I thought the other one was my forever path
Wide enough for wheelchairs and holding hands
Safe from falls
This one is crooked and cracked
I'm safe from falling
No I'm safe from being pushed or dragged
I think I'm home

I wanted to drink
So I didn't
I wanted to sleep
But I couldn't
I wanted to name my emotions
Instead I cried

I see what I've been doing wrong
Sitting inside working on the nothingness
of moving in
Boxes moved from one spot to the next
Forgetting to step outside
To take a deep breath of fresh air
So busy worrying I forgot to live
Smile in gratitude
Haven't sang
Haven't wrote
Haven't
Haven't begun to live
To believe I was free

'Mind your head' the sign said
I laughed out loud as I snapped a picture
It hung over the doorway
It still held several meanings for me
I traveled all this way and the first thing I see
Just happens to be this sign here
A warped piece of wood
Etched with
Mind Your Head
As if it knew my thoughts were out of control
I thought of signs asking parents
to mind their children
Our thoughts really can be like little ones
Impatient
Unruly
Just a little naughty
Impish
Loving
Never still

Unraveling
What a fabulous word
Unraveling
That's the word used to describe you
I am not responsible for that
I left because of that
Unraveling
Our relationship has been unraveling since
our wedding day
It all began before the quarantine
The pandemic is not to blame
The boredom was not to blame
Unraveling
That's what I'm doing
Unraveling all the lies
There were no truths
Unraveling the sadness from the anger
Even as the love remains

I never thought I had it in me
All these traits people told me
I saw only what my guilt-filled eyes could show me
Surviving somehow meant I did someone wrong
So often I did choose me over another
And the guilt just stomped me down
Today I looked into my boys' eyes
and knew that my surviving couldn't be wrong
For they are here
Which can only mean
I was meant to be
Strong and Resilient

It's been 40 years since I've had to flee
in the middle of the night.
It's been 40 years since I've had to live in a car,
grateful for that car.
It's been 40 years since I had no shoes.
How long will it be until I believe things have
changed?
How long will it be until I see the reality of now?
How long will it be until I stop hoarding food?
How long will it be until I stop hiding cash
all through the house?
How long will it take to stop seeing myself
as that destitute child?
How long will it take
for the fear of losing it all go away?

I can't keep sleeping
I can't keep drinking
I can't keep thinking
All these feelings
I can't keep wondering
I can't keep going back over and over
I can't keep still
All these feelings
I can't keep smoking
I can't keep hiding from myself and others
I can't keep my dreams at bay
All these feelings

You were swimming in poison
That's what I was told
Didn't believe it for the longest time
Those first steps out
Felt the air burn my skin
Didn't think I could breathe
It all made me ache
My heart was breaking
Now that I am fully out of the pool
No longer in that poison
No longer burning aching or breaking
My eyes have opened along with my lungs
Nothing to stop me from seeing my truth
I was swimming in poison

Conversations in my head
Perfectly put together words
Perfectly said for perfect impact
Everything I ever wanted to say to you
I uttered nothing in your presence
Scared into silence
Now laying in the dark instead of sleeping
I fantasize standing tall
Looking straight into your eyes
And saying it all
Letting it all go
The dreams and the wishes of a future
That was never going to happen
Letting it all go
I see the reality
Of what was and what is and what will be
Letting it all go I finally sleep

He's not taking anything from me
I've decided
I won't let him
I'll take the whole state
I wanted it first anyhow
He will say he has no where
That's his choice
He chose
Not me
I want the whole damn state
It's mine
The cacti and canyons
The desert
If I have to claim it I will
Florence
Mine
Camelback Inn
Mine
Murphy
All mine
My ancestry my love my home

I got a tree
I didn't last year
Hung their stockings
I didn't last year
Even bought them a few gifts
I didn't last year
I believe we are going to be ok
I didn't last year

I am sensitive not fragile
I am not weak
I cry and feel deeply
I am not weak
I process out loud
I am not weak

I've been begging from the get go
I see now the story I've written
I see it all so clearly
How much I beg
I begged for life while life's blood drained from you
I begged Starr to stop
I think I begged every day
So it makes sense that I would just
keep on begging
Begged to be left alone
Begged for it to be just a hug
I begged for you all to keep me
I begged and begged
I've begged so much now I look for opportunities
You were on your way out when I was on my way in
I begged for you to like me
I begged for acceptance from people
who didn't know I was begging
Didn't understand the need
I see my eagerness to be all that anyone wanted me
to be has left me with just one skill on my resume
I am ending my Beggars' Story this night
I beg of myself

Tomorrow
I will wake up
I will make breakfast
I will brush my teeth and wash my face
I will dress
I will do all the things I did
when I woke up for my boys
I will do all those things
Without my boys
Just for me

Alone

Aloneness

A hollow ache bouncing in the bottom of my stomach

and the whole of my heart

Stops my breath

The orphanage brought that same aloneness

Days of it

Beautiful sun filled days

Blue cloudless sky days

Children all around me and I still felt the same days

Here I sit in the middle of my sanctuary

aching with the day full of

Aloneness

I have a body

I have a soul

I have a mind

What else do I have?

I have love for my children

For my family

I have an endless stream of thoughts and feelings

Do I have a heart?

Do I have a brain?

I have a life

I have a view

Do I have success?

I have aches and pains

I have plans and dreams

Is that my heart or my soul?

What would it mean if it were true
To be ugly or fat aren't reasons to be this frozen
This scared to go out in public
What would it mean if I am
Does that make me hated or less than
Make me unworthy
Unable to laugh and enjoy
Does life not still happen even tho I am ugly and fat
I am acceptable now not soon
Not once I've done XYZ
Now
At this weight with this face

I'm emotional today
I can already feel the tears building in my chest
A tidal wave will be coming
Just don't know when

I wasn't meant to be
It really would seem
We've all heard the stats on below poverty living
The drugs the crime the heartache
The dead ends
Yet here I am
I made it out of her womb
I made it out of the ghetto
I made it out of my own thinking
The work was done to have a self
To have a home and children
To have a life

I spent the day with my son
He's driving and finally enjoying it
Had the honor of listening to his dreams
His tentative 5 year plan
We laughed and made eggs
Then off he went to the rest of his life

I watched the sun set tonight
Reflecting on all of this
I sliced my wrists, hung myself and even od'd
all because I thought I'd never have any of today
At 23 I thought my life was over
I couldn't see a future of any kind
On a locked down unit for I don't know how long
I thought it would be forever
I thought I was done

I thought I was done
I chuckle at the thought as I snap a pic of the sky
Done at 23

I looked up one day and realized where I was

I am a child
I am scared of shadows and noises in the night
I am an old woman
I am beautiful without paint and garland
I am middle aged
Wider every minute still sexually aware
I am ageless
A star being without limits
Perimeters are just words
Numbers on a sheet
I am everyone and everything
Time does not exist
Humans need it
Like air to breathe
I am a star being without limits
I can heal without touching
I can know without seeing
I can see without eyes
I am a star being
My mission is done
Another has begun
Loving and being become one
I am more than this body
I am less than this air
Did I mention I am a star being

I love to read

I love to write

I love to learn but not for a grade

I love Arizona

I love my boys

I love to think myself a butterfly

Fearless to change

A cowboy

Rugged and capable

I hate being frozen
Stuck somewhere in between
Not quite here
Yet not back there
My body doesn't know which place to choose
My mind doesn't either
Random thoughts of logic
Run ticker tape thru
Jumbled up with feelings
It's all too confusing
I just freeze
Like an animal playing dead
Maybe if I'm still enough the pain will go away
Maybe if I'm still enough no one will see me
Invisible has to be the safest
But that was long ago
I'm safe now aren't I?
No need to freeze
I am safe now
I can choose to be safe from now on

These are the stars I looked upon and thought
"I'll never be free"

Barefoot
I walked barefoot down a dusty sidewalk
My bloody footprint leaving a trail
I walked barefoot on cold basement concrete
I walked barefoot on bare wooden floors
and cracked linoleum
I walked barefoot in grocery stores
way past the age of 3
I walked barefoot in Ohio Kentucky and Nebraska
I walked barefoot on the plane today
I walk barefoot now
Not because I don't have shoes
But because I have the choice

I was rejected
Turned away while embraced
A fuck you with a smile
I felt my heart shrink a little
Go back in time to the orphanage
Rejected
That was my story
I told myself every day
Not wanted
Not loved
Not seen

I smiled into the sun today
Closed my eyes to the breeze
Wildflowers filling my nose
I'm changing my story
From rejection to freedom

I bought earrings today from a Navajo woman
They are like little suns dangling from my ears
When I move my head they sway
It makes me smile
They make me smile
Radiating love just like the sun rays
I watched as she began a bracelet
Everything in the shop she made
with her own hands
She herself as bright as the sun as we laughed
while I tried to say her name

I walked off the plane in Waco
The wind came whipping through
It reminded me of Kansas
How the wind came across the prairie
Swirls around and around
Nothing to do but feel the glee
Confirmation of being alive
Hello in the most beautiful way

There will be no guns today
No need to crawl into a corner to hide
There won't even be a chair thrown
Instead let us agree to be mad
And maybe even sad!
There will be no weapons of any sort
No slapping or hitting
Not even a bite
Let us each see the whites of each other's eyes
and not charge forward
Even if we can't hug
Let us smile and sit and have
the whole scene of destruction in our heads
Only metaphorical murders will occur
Try not to laugh out loud tho
This is a play for just us two

I am a survivor
I am a loser
I am a taker
I am a trampler
I survived
Someone didn't
I lived
Someone didn't
I got my way
Someone didn't
I have it all
Someone doesn't

I never thought I'd be sitting here
Taking inventory of a blessed life
I never was an optimist
Yet here I sit
Watching the Arizona sunset
Breathing in the coldness of this desert landscape
The cooing mingled with my sons' voices
Mummy Mountain in the distance
Time for dinner
Family dinner
In our kitchen
Filled with love

There was a time in this life when all I wanted
was to be chosen
Someones to call mom and dad
There was a time in this life when all I wanted
was no fence between me and the rest
The chance to touch the leaves beyond my reach
There was a time in this life when
the ache was so great it swallowed me whole
I hung like a big full moon in the depths of darkness
There was a time in this life when all I wanted
was to disappear
Walk invisible upon the earth
There was a time in this life when I wanted
my voice to split the scene in half
Stop time with my words Feel heard beyond ears
There was a time in this life when I thought
I'd never have a life
A life of my own
To fly To soar
To love

One thing I know for certain
I never thought I'd be in this spot
on the path of my life's journey
Walking my path I jumped to certain conclusions
Barefoot and dead at 28 were my givens
45 and barefoot for enjoyment was never the plan
The path I'm on I've been on since birth
This time around at least
Plopped right down on the dirt
Our God is so good
He picked the perfect path for me
Busy and barren
Clean and cluttered
Winding and straight
All the steps were for a reason
The shady and the sunny
My lessons are mine
My soul's work
Google Earth gave me the overview of my path
I can see from the beginning to the end
The path like branches leading to
endless possibilities

I know for certain I don't care what I look like
on this path
I am just grateful to have a journey
Maybe something of my very own

If I were a cowboy
I'd wear spurs on my boots
Jeans snug to my body
Shirt tucked in with a big belt buckle
Cowboy hat low on my head
Ride a horse like we were one
Fly along with the wind whipping my hair

Oh I feel the desert calling me home
The ruggedness of this landscape
breathes into my soul
Smell the sage and mesquite
Hear the wind as it whips thru me
Surrounds me as tho hugging me
Time does not exist here
Every moment is everywhere all at once
Suspending me in contentment
Calm as I ride this wave of welcome
Laughter erupting as the wave crashes

I want

I've hated that yearning inside since I was very little
It started with wanting food so badly
it was all I could think about
I tried to shove aside this desire
Not truly knowing the difference between
want and need
It's all a yearning inside that aches in every bone
I try not to want anything
Keep it simple and maybe the universe won't
take it away
As I have become more free in my thinking
all these wants come bubbling back up inside
I sit here in the yard I've wanted
in the state that I've wanted while the boys
I've wanted are at school and start my lists of wants

I want

To go ride a horse

To sew

To bake gluten-free yumminess

To touch the red rocks as I sing thank you

To learn new things

To look everyone in the eye

To write from the heart

To see my beauty and strength

To fly like in my dreams

To pass on love

I want a yard
A back yard
A place for all 3 totem poles
A pool
Doesn't have to have a rock slide but
definitely want a water "feature"
Fuck never thought I'd use that word!
Lots of patio
Shade and direct sunlight
Don't need grass Maybe some dirt
Trees Palm and otherwise
I wouldn't mind a cactus or two
Places to do my pranas
Stretches and hellos to God
Ability to chant and play the native drums
and do moon rituals without anyone in the way

I went to a dark place
Maybe that is good
Now I can truly see the light
All my demons came forth
Reared their ugly heads
I looked them all in the eyes
Even thanked them

I want a room Maybe two
Lots of windows
Lots of sunlight
All full of trees Plants Flowers
I want to have fun growing trees from seeds
From saplings too
Crystals everywhere
Murphys everywhere
I want to grow an almond tree
The beautiful white flowers
A sunflower
As tall as the ones in Kansas
Oh a cherry blossom tree
A magnolia tree
Herbs
Michigan sweet corn
My own strawberries

A good country song line
I remember the desperation though
and stop the chuckling
The longing for something I didn't have
It hits me like a tidal wave
The longing
The longing for
A mom and dad
A home
Acceptance
A love that doesn't end
I wipe my tears snap another photo
Smile as I think of what I gave my boys
My boys
They have all those things I longed for
And I think so much more
I am grateful
Just so grateful

If it takes eyebrows then tint them
If it takes long nails then manicure them
If it takes make up or hair gel or both
then paint yourself more gorgeous
If it takes braids and long skirts
Then twist those fingers
Wear those skirts
Weave those blankets that tell your history
Pass them on to make more history
Your wings are there
Untethered
Unused
Spread them
They will naturally soar

Power

Pulse
Pull

Own
Own

Win
War

Ego
Ever

Rise
Riot

Truth is my power
Love is my power
Light is my power
Balance is my power

I want to ride a horse like a real cowboy
Write a book
Learn Navajo
Help
Love all
Plant
Sing and chant
Dance and laugh everyday
Greet the sun with a smile
Be an old crone that walks all the worlds
Grow my hair long long long
Read...everything

In gratitude
Thank you God for this day
The sun rising to greet us
The warmth on our faces
Thank you God for this day
This meeting
This chance to be together
Thank you God for this day
Bringing our hearts together
To bring out the best in ourselves and each other
To make a difference
Thank you God for this day

All the potential

All the things I thought you would take away
I have now
All the things I wanted to do some day
I am doing now
All that I hoped to be some day
I am now

We need something to believe in
It almost seems it doesn't matter what it even is
Just something
Stock car racing
Jesus
A way of life
Something that said
This is why I'm doing what I'm doing
This is why I rise every day with a smile on my face

Today I was a sheep
Sure footed
Sturdy on the rugged rocks and turf
I can feel the cool earth beneath me
I am capable
I am strong
I am the earth
As I am the sheep

We've landed

We've landed

My heart has filled with the mesquite trees and
flowers

I'm home

I'm home

I never want to leave again

My skin feels the lack of moisture

My bones too

I sing out THANK YOU

I can dance and soar

This is not a dream

This is home

This is Arizona

I am a drummer
I am a chanter
I am in love with the rhythm
I am a storyteller oral and written
I am a keeper of history
I am in love with the rhythm
I am a warrior
I am a survivor
I am in love with the rhythm
I am a seeker
I am a knower
I am in love with the rhythm
I am a lover of flesh, food and spirit
I am a human
I am after all in love with the rhythm

I miss him
I miss him like never before
It must be the facts
This time no one here but me
It's as tho there has never been enough
time with them
And now it's too late
It's not true
That's just the feelings
We spent the weekend
binge watching anime shows
The most time together in months
It all hurts
My heart
My head
The memories
The love

I asked the Lord for guidance
My stumbling must stop
Chuckling with such love and patience
he quietly asked me
Why do you stumble?
Because I'm just not good enough I reply
Such a simple question child
Why do you stumble?
I breathed in his love and burst out laughing
Of course! I stumble because I am not looking!
I stumble because I am moving too fast!
I bow in wonderment and gratitude

What if everything she is saying is true?
Would it silence that voice in my head?
Would it erase the story written by me?
(Continued by me)
Will this change anything? Everything?

I think I thought I could starve myself back
to Tina Lynch
Back to 7 years old
Back to pickable
What am I if I'm not the orphan?
What am I if I'm not the scrawny survivor?
What am I now?